E S T A T E   P U B L

T E L F O

C000172394

Shawbirch	Leegomery		
4 5	6 7	Muxton 8 9	
Admaston	Hortonwood	Donnington	
Wrockwardine 10 11 Wellington	Hadley 12 13 Ketley	Redhill 14 15 Oakengates	
	Lawley 16 17 Dawley	3 TELFORD CENTRE 19 18 Stafford Park	
	Woodside 20 21 Coalbrookdale	Stirchley 22 23 Madeley Halesfield	
	Ironbridge 24 25 Broseley	26 Coalport	

ROAD MAP — **Page 2**

TELFORD ENLARGED TOWN CENTRE — **Page 3**

STREET INDEX — **Page 27**

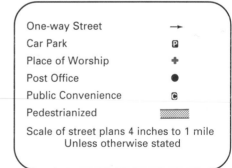

Every effort has been made to verify the
accuracy of information in this book
but the publishers cannot accept
responsibility for expense or loss caused
by any error or omission. Information
that will be of assistance to the user of
the maps will be welcomed.

The representation of a road, track or
footpath on the maps in this atlas is no
evidence of the existence of a right of way.

One-way Street   →
Car Park   🅿
Place of Worship   ✛
Post Office   ●
Public Convenience   🄲
Pedestrianized   ▨

Scale of street plans 4 inches to 1 mile
Unless otherwise stated

Street plans prepared and published by ESTATE PUBLICATIONS, Bridewell House,
TENTERDEN, KENT, and based upon the ORDNANCE SURVEY mapping with the
permission of The Controller of H. M. Stationery Office.

The publishers acknowledge the co-operation of the local
authorities of towns represented in this atlas.

© Estate Publications 319 F   ISBN 0 86084 815 9   © Crown Copyright 398713

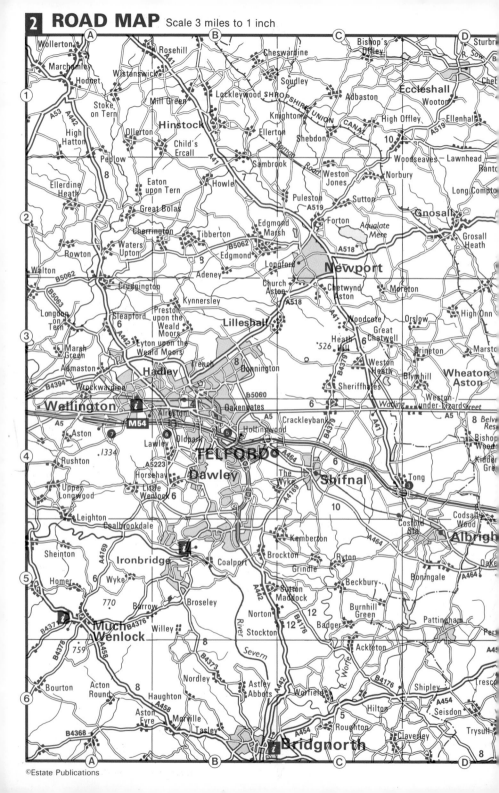

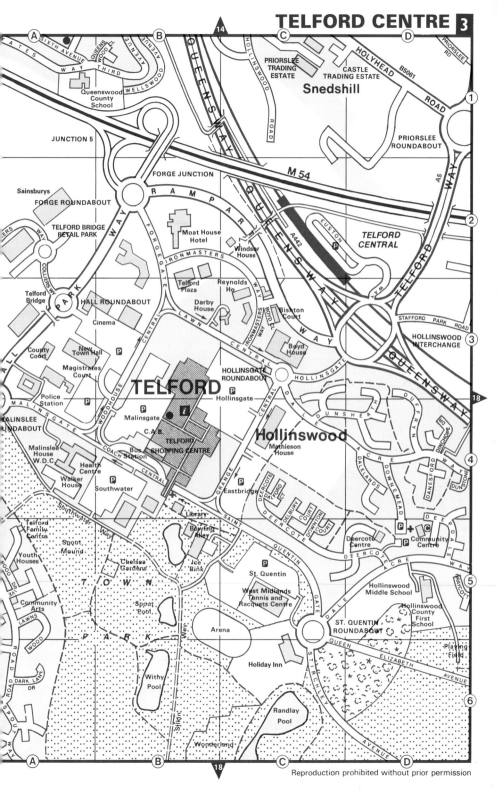

Reproduction prohibited without prior permission

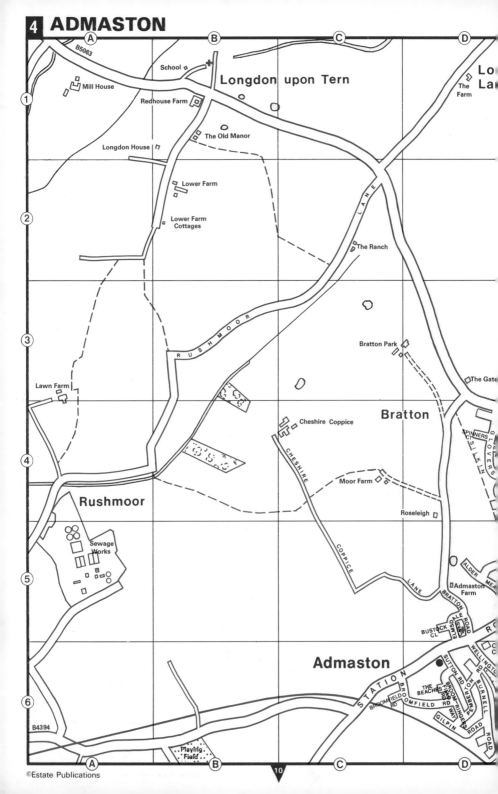

4 ADMASTON

B5063

Mill House

School

Longdon upon Tern

The Farm

Lo
La

Redhouse Farm

The Old Manor

Longdon House

Lower Farm

Lower Farm
Cottages

The Ranch

LANE

RUSHMOOR

Bratton Park

The Gate

Lawn Farm

Cheshire Coppice

Bratton

SPINNERS
CL

GLOVERS
IN

CHESHIRE

Moor Farm

Rushmoor

Roseleigh

COPPICE

Sewage
Works

ALDER
MEA

LANE

BRATTON

Admaston
Farm

BUSTOCK
CL

ELMSDALE
ROAD

WELL

NOTL

R

Admaston

STATION

SUTTON RD

THE
BEACHES

BROOMFIELD
BROOMFIELD RD

RINGES

BURNELL

EMBE
WAY

ROAD

GILPIN
ROAD

BURNELL
ROAD

Playing
Field

©Estate Publications

B4394

Eyton Moor

New Rookery

Hurley Brook

Shropshire Union Canal (disused)

Eyton Lock

Eyton upon the Weald Moors

Eyton House

Eyton Hall

Den Wood House

Wheelwright Covert

Longpit Coppice

Eyton Farm

Shawbirch

Hopkins Hth

Harrington Hth

Forest Cl

Arrow Way

Guisbourne Av

Rough Pits

Mere Gro

Leeses Mdw

Gainsborough Road

Buttso

Glade

Oakfield Road

Span Mdw

Meadow

Cole Rd

Aspen

Chestnut Way

Fallow Rd

Covert Ct

Acorn Wy

Constable Wy

Lowry Cl

Embranut Cl

Monet

WBIRCH ROAD

ROAD

Comm Centre

Quail Cl

Swan Gate

Lake Gate

Plover Gate

Swift Gate

Marsh Mdw Cl

Coch Mdw

Boulevard

McCormick

Harley

Tee

St Agathas Cl

St Julians Cl

Fernwood Cl

Condover Wy

Green Wy

Umbers Cl

St Marks Cl

School

Tee Lake

Dothill

Bush Cl

Rise

Whitchurch Cl

St Lawrence Cl

St Marks Cl

Teme Rd

Morville Dr

Clun Av

Avenue Rd

Severn Rd

Stokesay Rd

Breidden Pl

Dothill Pool

Dothill County Schools

Grinshill Cl

Flats

Fern

Severn Way

Meese Cl

Training Centre

Dee Close

Haughmond Wy

Eyton Cl

Apley Cl

Playing Field

College

Playing Field

SHAWBIRCH ROUNDABOUT

QUEENSWAY

A442

WHITCHURCH

Pool Wood

Factory

Apley Pool

Pump Wood

Apley Park

Apley Home Farm

Apley Castle

CASTLE

APLEY

Fish Ponds

SILKIN WAY

THE PRINCESS ROYAL (TELFORD DISTRICT GENERAL) HOSPITAL

Accident & Emergency Entrance

Main Entrance

DRIVE

A5223

APLEY R/BOUT

GRAINGER DRIVE

KINGSHMER CL

STONECHAT CL

SANDPIPER CL

BARTRIDGE CL

JAY

Reproduction prohibited without prior permission

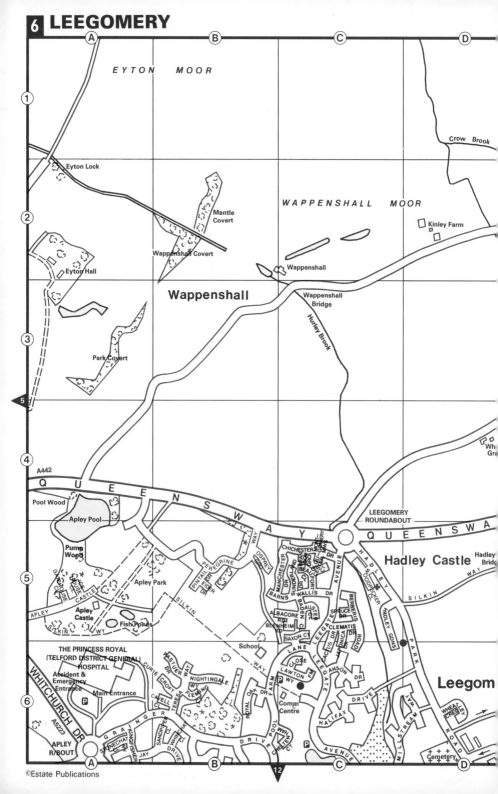

EYTON MOOR

Eyton Lock

Mantle Covert

WAPPENSHALL MOOR

Kinley Farm

Wappenshall Covert

Eyton Hall

Wappenshall

Wappenshall

Wappenshall Bridge

Hurley Brook

Park Covert

Crow Brook

A442

QUEENSWAY

Pool Wood

Apley Pool

Pump Wood

LEEGOMERY ROUNDABOUT

QUEENSWA

Hadley Castle

Hadley Bridg

SILKIN

Apley Park

PINTAIL DR

PEREGRINE

OSPREY

WAY

CHICHESTER

MANCHESTER

SUNDERLAND

BEAUFORT

DR

AVENUE

HADLEY

WOODPECKER

SILKIN

Apley Castle

CASTLE

SILKIN WY

APLEY

Fish Ponds

SILKIN

BARNS

WALLIS

DR

BERBERIS

HADLEY GDNS

PARK

ALBACORE

BADEN

SPRUCE DR

BLENHEIM

SAXON CT

LEEGATE

CACTUS DR

RD

CLEMATIS

VERONICA

ROAD

School

THE PRINCESS ROYAL
(TELFORD DISTRICT GENERAL)
HOSPITAL

Accident &
Emergency
Entrance

Main Entrance

P

WHITCHURCH DR

A5223

APLEY
R/BOUT

CURIE

PASTUER WAY

CROFT

TERESA

FLEMING

CAVELL

NIGHTINGALE

WY

WAY

FARM

ROYAL OAK

DR

GRAINGER

SANDRINE

SANDFORD

KINGFISHER

JAY

DRIVE

NECHAT CL

WHIMBREL

WAY

LANE

LAWTON WY

LEEGATE

ANSON

DR

ROSE

HALIFAX

DRIVE

Comm
Centre

CHEETHAM CT

POOL

DRIVE

AVENUE

MILLSTREAM

WAY

Hadley Castle

Leegom

WHEAT CREST

ROAD

Cemetery

Wh
Gra

A

B

C

D

1

2

3

4

5

6

©Estate Publications

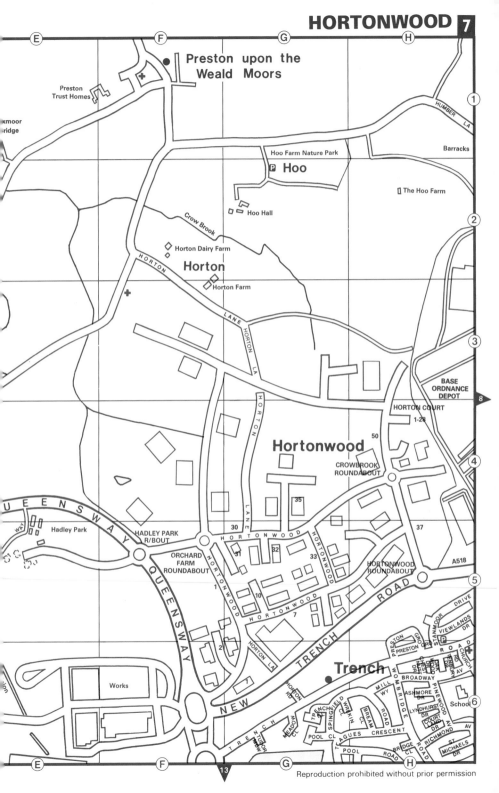

Preston Trust Homes

xmoor ridge

Preston upon the Weald Moors

Hoo Farm Nature Park

P **Hoo**

Barracks

The Hoo Farm

Crow Brook

◇ Horton Dairy Farm

Horton

HORTON

◇ Horton Farm

LANE

HORTON LA

Hoo Hall

BASE ORDNANCE DEPOT

HORTON COURT
1-28

50

Hortonwood

CROWBROOK ROUNDABOUT

HORTON LANE

HADLEY PARK R/BOUT

Hadley Park

QUEENSWAY

WY

ORCHARD FARM ROUNDABOUT

35

30

HORTONWOOD

31

32

33

37

HORTONWOOD ROUNDABOUT

A518

HORTONWOOD

1

10

7

HORTON LA

2

7

HORTONWOOD

QUEENSWAY

Works

NEW

TRENCH

ROAD

Trench

PRESTON GRO

PRESTON

PINEWOOD DRIVE

VIEWLANDS DR

ROAD

WOMBRIDGE ROAD

BROADWAY

ASHMORE DR

LYNDHURST DR

PINEWOOD DR

COURT LANE

RICHMOND DR

CHURCH RD

TENBURY AV

School

ST MICHAELS DR

AV

MILL WY

BREAM ROAD

BRIDGE CL

RICHMOND DR

TRENCH

TRENCHFIELD

SPRINGFIELD

WREKIN

POOL CL

LAGUES CRESCENT

MEADOW CL

HORTON LA

POOL ROAD

TRENCH ROAD

NEW ROAD

13

Reproduction prohibited without prior permission

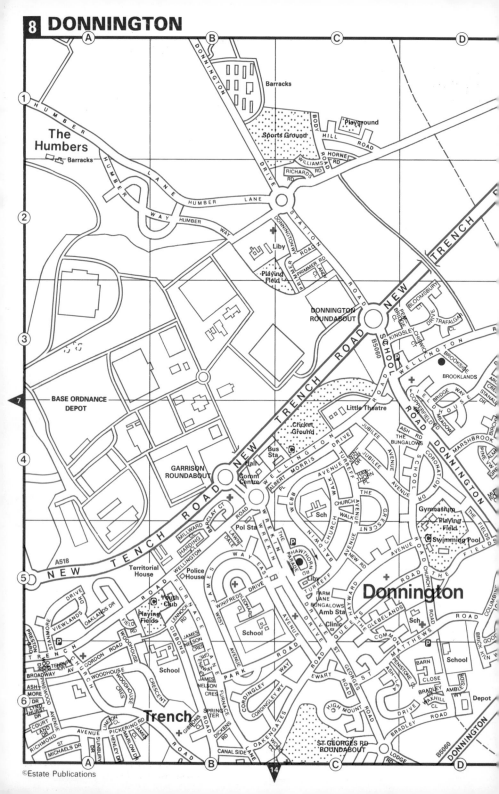

©Estate Publications

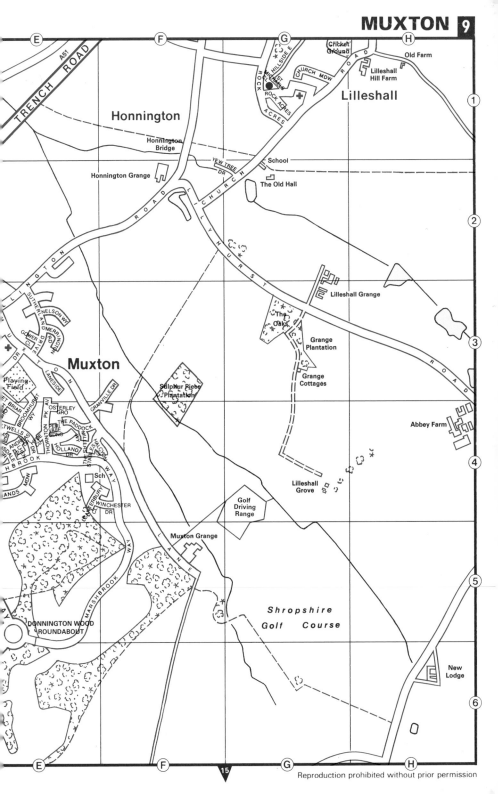

Lilleshall

Honnington

Muxton

Reproduction prohibited without prior permission

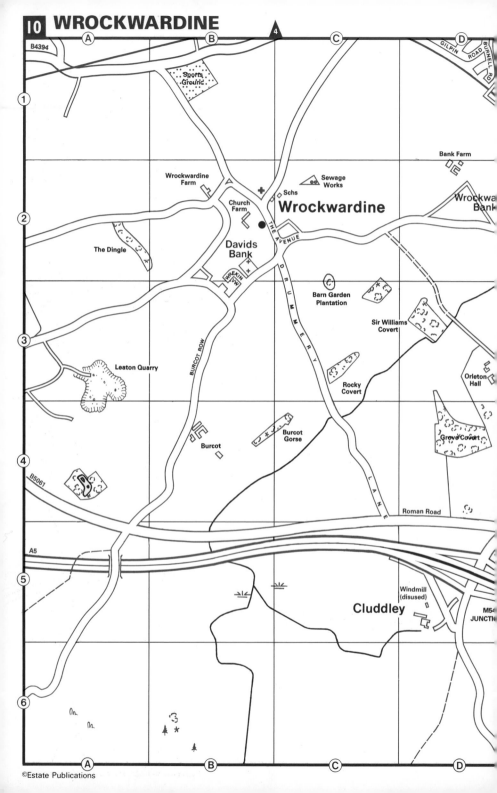

A B C D

B4394

Sports Ground

GILPIN ROAD
BURNELL RD

1

Bank Farm

Wrockwardine Farm

Sewage Works

Schs

Wrockwardine

Wrockwa Bank

Church Farm

2

The Dingle

Davids Bank

THE AVENUE

WREKIN ROW

Barn Garden Plantation

Sir Williams Covert

3

BURCOT ROW

Leaton Quarry

DRUMMERY

Rocky Covert

Orleton Hall

Burcot

Burcot Gorse

Grove Covert

4

B5061

LANE

Roman Road

A5

5

Windmill (disused)

Cluddley

M54 JUNCTIO

6

©Estate Publications

A B C D

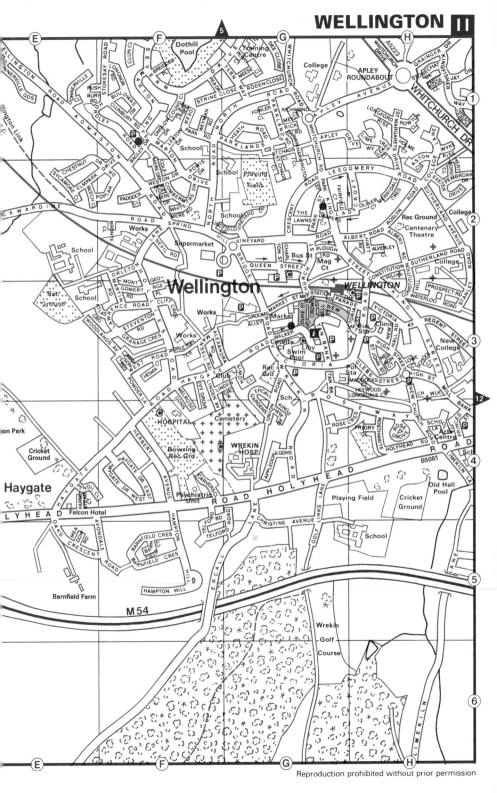

Reproduction prohibited without prior permission

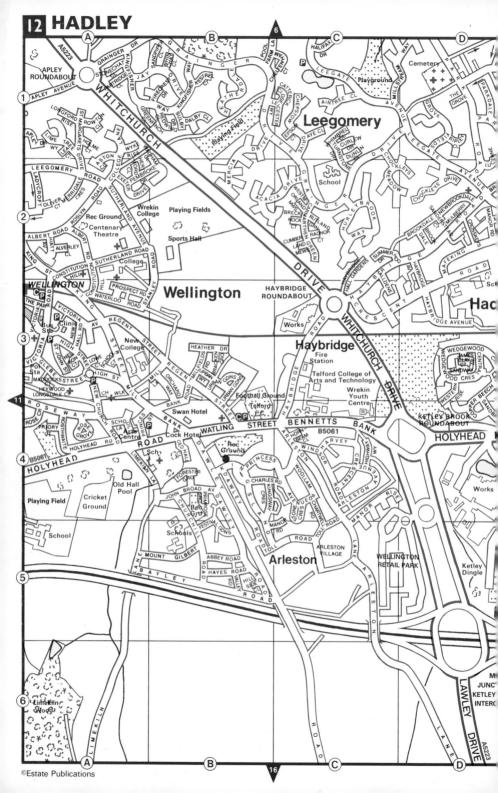

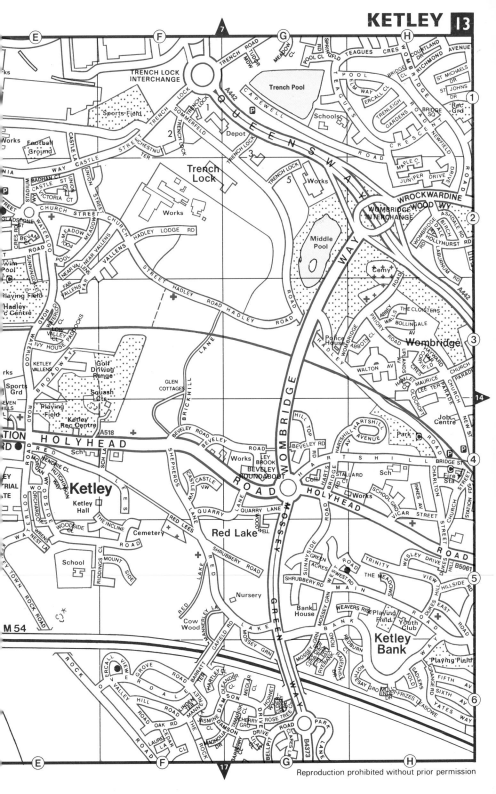

Reproduction prohibited without prior permission

14 OAKENGATES

©Estate Publications

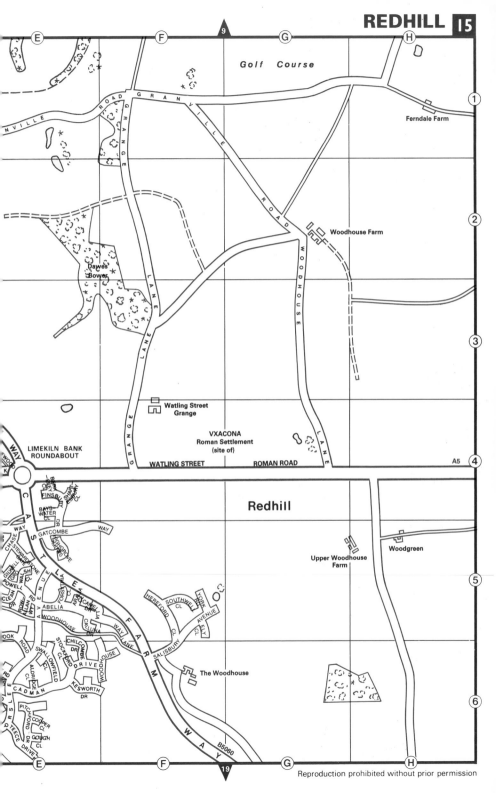

Golf Course

E F 9 G H

GRANVILLE ROAD

Ferndale Farm 1

Woodhouse Farm 2

Dawes Bower

WOODHOUSE LANE

LANE

3

Watling Street Grange

GRANGE LANE

LIMEKILN BANK ROUNDABOUT

VXACONA
Roman Settlement
(site of)

WATLING STREET   ROMAN ROAD   A5 4

WAY

FOLK

CASTLE WAY

Redhill

BERRY DR
FINSBURY CL
BAYSWATER CL
GATCOMBE WAY
CHASE WAY
STEWART STONE
GUNHILL DR
POWELL
CLEN
ROWE RD
ABELIA
WOODHOUSE
STOCKFORD CL
CHILCOMBE DR
SWALLOWFIELD
ALDRIDGE CL
CADMAN
KESWORTH DR
COOPER
PITCHFORD CL
GOUGH
HORSLEE
TEECE DRIVE
ROAD

Woodgreen

Upper Woodhouse Farm 5

HEREFORD CL
SOUTHWELL CL
YORK CL
CALUNA
FORSE
ARA CANEY DR
AVENUE
ELY PL
SALISBURY
FARM WAY LANE AVENUE

The Woodhouse

6

B5060

WAY

E F 19 G H

Reproduction prohibited without prior permission

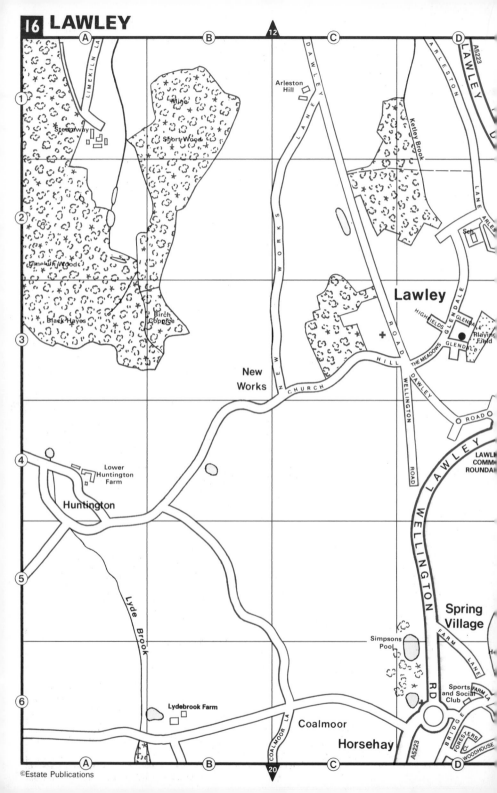

16 LAWLEY

©Estate Publications

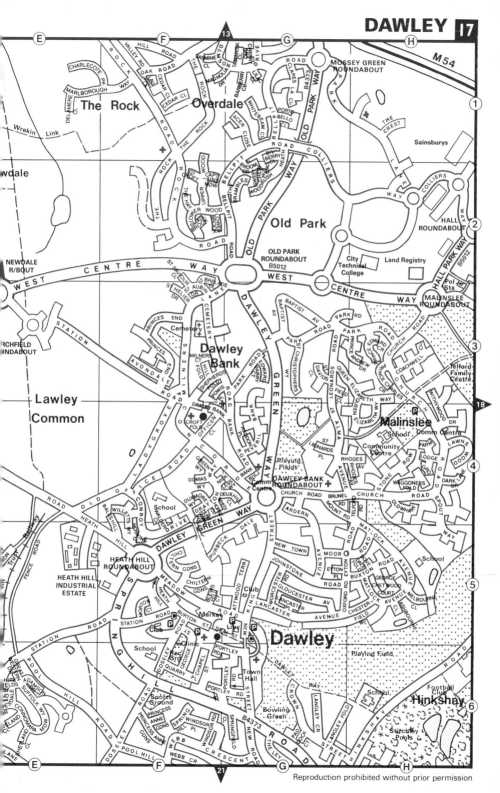

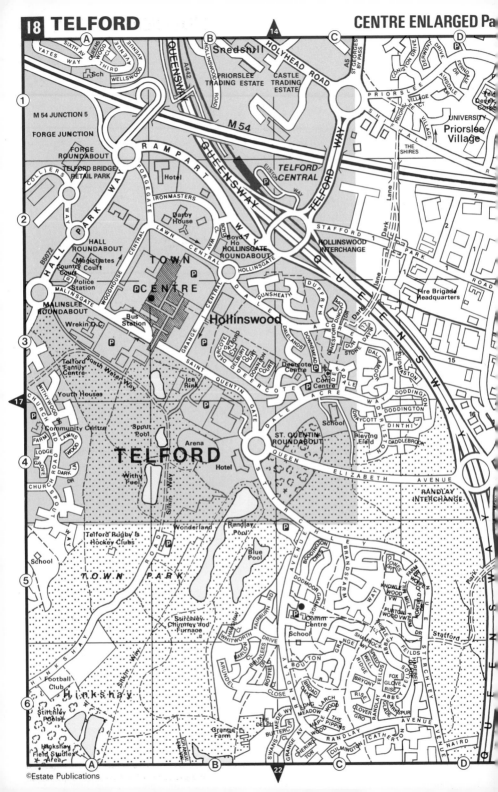

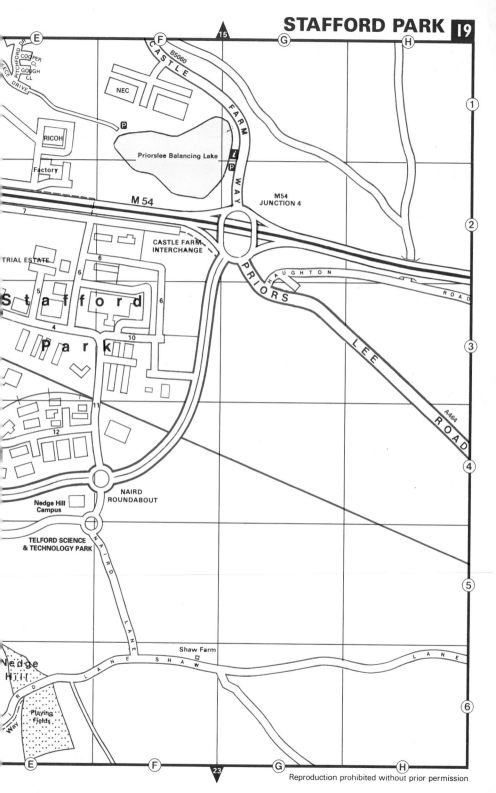

Reproduction prohibited without prior permission

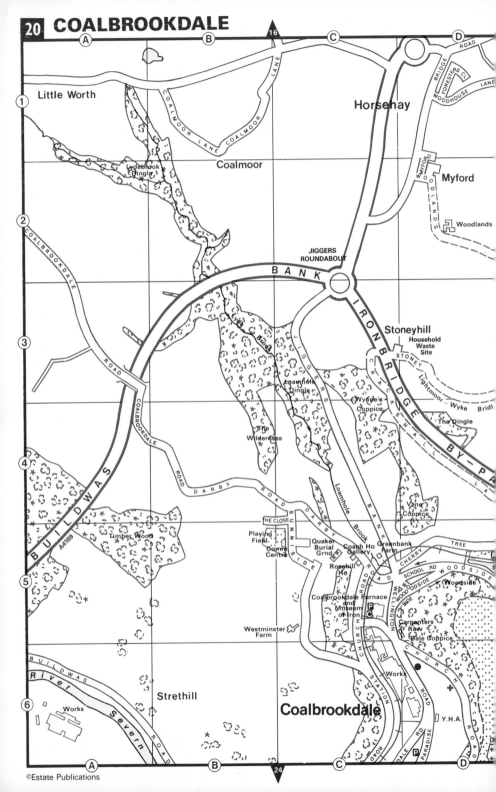

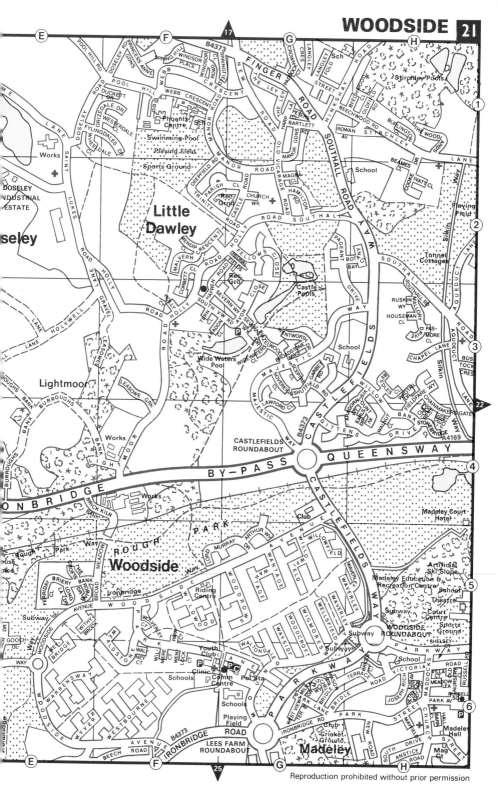

Reproduction prohibited without prior permission

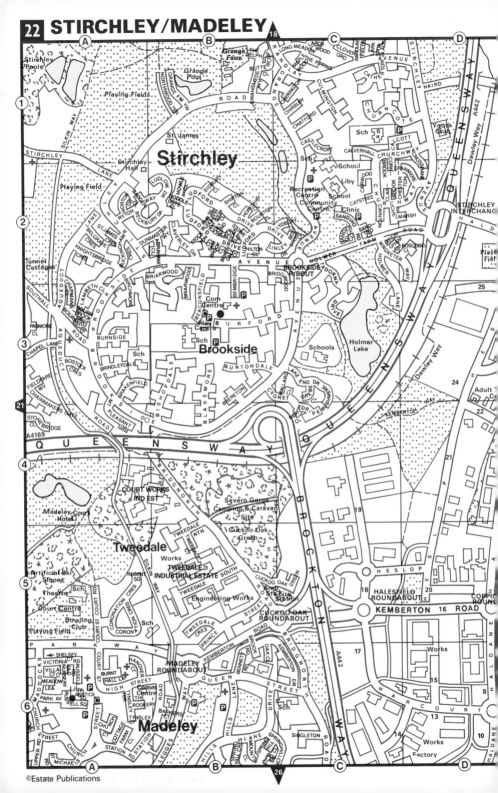

©Estate Publications

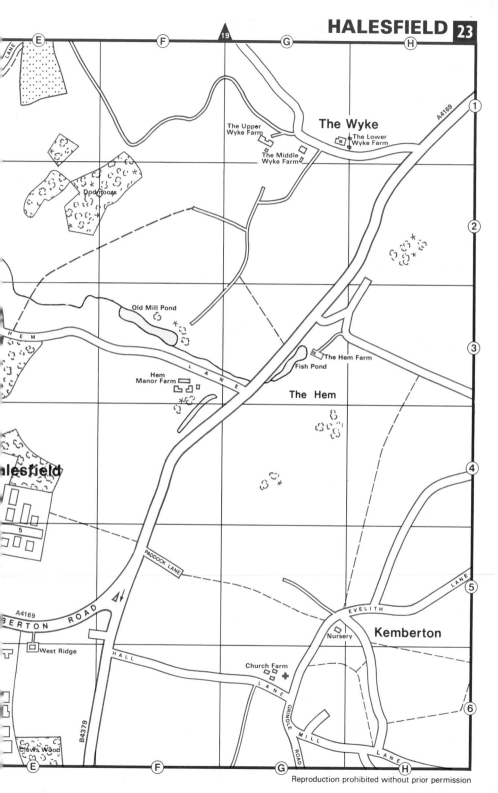

The Wyke

The Upper Wyke Farm

The Lower Wyke Farm

The Middle Wyke Farm

Doodmoors

Old Mill Pond

Hem Manor Farm

The Hem Farm

Fish Pond

The Hem

LANE

HEM

Halesfield

5

A4169

PADDOCK LANE

BERTON ROAD

West Ridge

HALL

LANE

B4379

Clews Wood

EVELITH

LANE

Kemberton

Nursery

Church Farm

GRINDLE MILL ROAD

LANE

Reproduction prohibited without prior permission

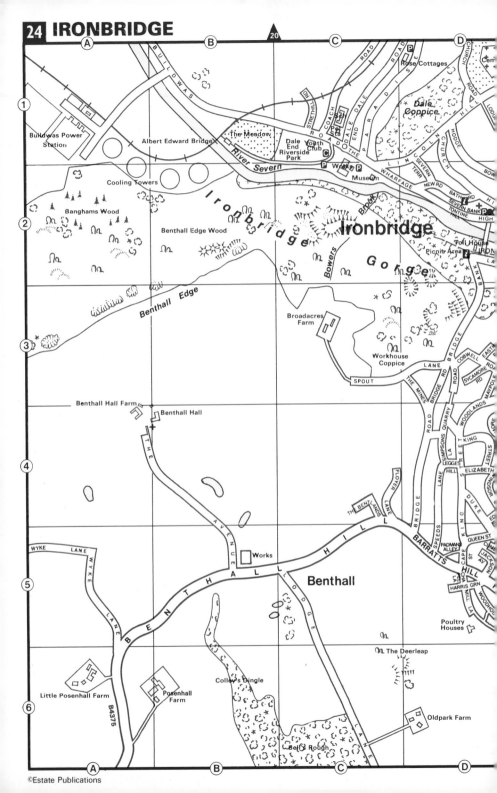

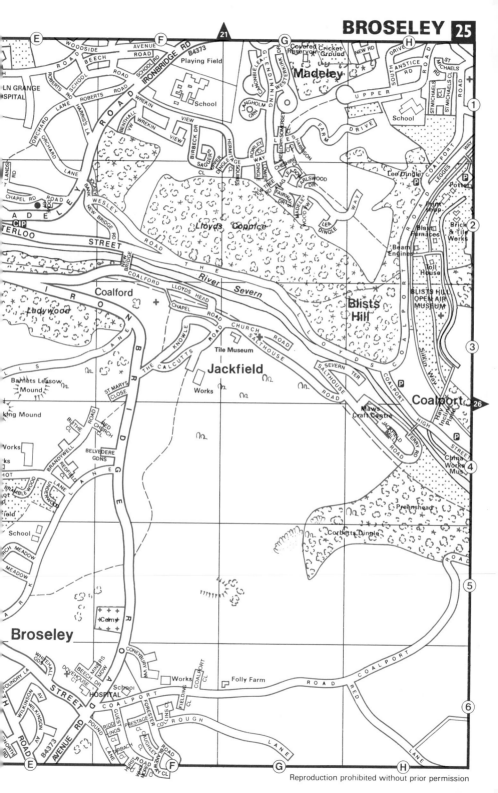

21

E F IRONBRIDGE RD G Covered Cricket NEW RD H
WOODSIDE B4373 Reservoir Ground
AVENUE School Playing Field SOUTH DRIVE ST MICHAELS
BEECH ROAD GLENDINNING ANSTICE
ROBERTS RD ROAD WESTERKIRK Madeley RD ST MICHAELS CL
LN GRANGE SCHOOL LANE CRONKBIELEA UPPER St MICHAELS 1
SPITAL ROBERTS ROAD WREKIN SOMERSET School
ORCHARD LANE HARRIS LA VIEW LANGHOLM CHELFORD FARM DRIVE
ORCHARD WREKIN BIRBECK DR GDN CHESHIRE
CHAPEL RD LANE ROAD VIEW SAGGERS CL DINGLE AGE HOUSES HARRISON Lee Dingle LEGGES WAY P Potter
BANK WESLEY THE DINGLE EARLSWOOD DR COALPORT WAY 2
ADELEY NEW BRIDGE HERMAN POWLEY FAIRWAY DR Flint
CIP WATERLOO STREET ROAD MADELEY LEA DINGLE Shop Blast Brick
NEW BRIDGE ROAD WOOD TOWN Furnaces & Tile
COALFORD ROAD River Severn Beam Works
Coalford LLOYDS HEAD Lloyds Coppice Engines Toll 2
Ladywood CHAPEL KNOWLE CHURCH ROAD House BLISTS HILL
I R O N ROAD SALTHOUSE Blists OPEN AIR
Barnets Leasow THE CALCUTTS Tile Museum L Hill MUSEUM 3
Mound ST MARYS CLOSE Works L O Y SILKIN WAY
king Mound BLITHE CL Jackfield SEVERN TER D S
Works RED CHURCH CL SALTHOUSE C Coalport 26
HOT BELVEDERE GDNS ROAD ROAD P HIGH
BRANDYWELL REDFIELD Maws JACKFIELD STREET
ield LANE LINDERWOOD Craft Centre MILL RD 4
School THE RIDGE LANE China
CHURCH MEADOW Works
MEADOW Preenshead
PARK 5
Cemy Corbetts Dingle
Broseley CONEYBURY VW
WHITEHALL MINERS ROAD
GDNS DOVEHOUSE CL MEADOW School Works COALPORT CL Folly Farm COALPORT ROAD RED 6
STREET CL HOSPITAL FIELDING CL ROUGH LANE LANE
WILKINSON AV COALPORT FORESTER CL COLLINS CL
FOUNDRY LA WILKINSON BEECH RD GUEST PRESTAGE CL
ROAD AV POUND RIDGE CL LINGS CL LAKEWAY CL
B4373 AVENUE RD LANE HURST BIRBACK ROAD
E F G H

Reproduction prohibited without prior permission

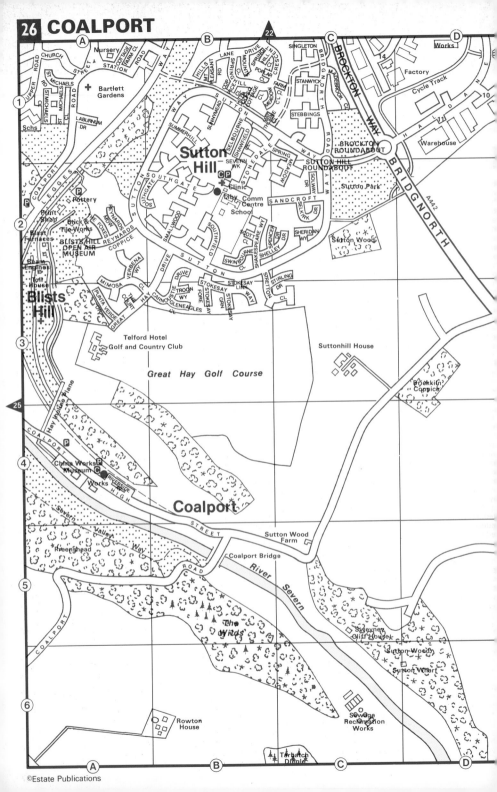

©Estate Publications

A - Z INDEX TO STREETS
with Postcodes

Index includes some names
which there is insufficient
ce on the maps. These names
preceded by an * and are
wed by the nearest adjoining
roughfare.

TELFORD

Street	Ref
Chapel Rd, Jackfield. TF8	25 F3
Chapel St, Dawley. TF4	17 F6
Chapel St, St Georges. TF2	14 C4
Chapel Ter. TF2	14 B1
Chapmans Clo. TF3	22 A3
Charlecote Park. TF3	17 E1
Charles Rd. TF1	12 B4
Charles St. TF2	14 B1
Charlton St, Oakengates. TF2	13 H4
Charlton St, Wellington. TF1	11 G2
Chartwell Rd. TF1	12 C4
Chatford. TF3	22 C1
Checkley La. TF2	14 D4
Chelmarsh. TF3	22 C2
Cheltenham Clo. TF1	6 C6
Chepstow Dri. TF1	12 C1
Cherington. TF3	22 C1
Cherry Gro. TF3	13 G6
Cherry Tree Hill. TF8	20 D5
Cherrybrook Dri. TF12	24 D4
Cheshire Clo. TF7	25 G2
Cheshire Coppice La. TF5	4 C4
Chesterfield Rd. TF4	17 H5
Chesterton. TF3	22 D2
Chestnut Dri, Trench. TF2	7 H6
Chestnut Dri, Wellington. TF1	11 E2
Chestnut Ter. TF1	13 F1
Chetwynd Clo. TF3	22 B2
Chichester Dri. TF1	6 C5
Chilcombe Dri. TF2	15 E6
Chiltern Gdns. TF4	17 F5
Chirbury. TF3	22 C1
Chiswick Ct. TF2	8 D3
Chockleys Dri. TF1	12 D2
Chockleys Meadow. TF1	12 C2
Christine Av. TF1	11 G4
Church Ct. TF7	22 A6
Church Hill, Ironbridge. TF8	24 D1
Church Hill, Lawley. TF6	16 C3
Church Meadow. TF10	9 G1
Church Par. TF2	14 A3
Church Rd, Coalbrookdale. TF8	20 D6
Church Rd, Dawley. TF4	17 G4
Church Rd, Donnington. TF2	8 D5
Church Rd, Lilleshall. TF10	9 F2
Church Rd, Snedshill. TF2	14 B6
Church Rd, Trench. TF2	8 A6
Church St, Broseley. TF12	25 E5
Church St, Hadley. TF1	13 E2
Church St, Madeley. TF7	21 H6
Church St, Oakengates. TF2	14 A4
Church St, St Georges. TF2	14 C4
Church St, Wellington. TF1	11 G2
Church Walk, Donnington. TF2	8 C4
Church Walk, Little Dawley. TF4	21 G2
Church Walk, Wellington. TF1	11 H3
Churchill Dri. TF2	14 A5
Churchill Rd. TF1	12 B4
Churchward Clo. TF2	15 E5
Churchway. TF3	22 C2
Churncote. TF3	22 C1
Clanbrook. TF3	22 C2
Clares La. TF3	13 G6
Clares Lane Clo. TF3	17 G1
Claverley Dri. TF3	22 B2
*Clee Ct, Breidden Pl. TF1	5 F6
Clematis Dri. TF1	6 C5
Cleveland Clo. TF4	17 E6
Clift Cres. TF1	11 F3
Clover Gro. TF3	18 C6
*Clowes Dri, Knowle Wood View. TF3	18 C5
Clun Clo. TF1	5 F6
Clunbury Rd. TF1	11 F1
Clydesdale Dri. TF4	17 E6
Coach Central. TF3	3 B4
Coach Rd. TF8	24 C1
Coachman Meadow. TF1	5 F5
Coachwell Clo. TF3	3 A4
Coalbrookdale Rd. TF8	20 A2
Coalford. TF8	25 F2
Coalmoor La. TF4	20 B1
Coalport Clo. TF12	25 F6
Coalport High St. TF8	26 A4
Coalport Rd, Broseley. TF12	25 F6
Coalport Rd, Broseley.TF7	25 H3
Cobwell Rd. TF12	24 D3
Cockshot La. TF12	24 D5
Cockshutt Rd. TF2	14 B4
Colemere Dri. TF1	11 F2
College La. TF1	12 A2
Collett Way. TF2	14 D5
Colliers Way. TF3	3 A2
Collins Clo. TF12	25 F6
Columbine Way. TF2	8 D5
Combermere Dri. TF1	11 F2
Commercial Way. TF2	14 A4
Concorde. TF4	17 F4
Coney Green Way. TF1	5 G5
Coneybury Vw. TF12	25 F6
Coniston Dri. TF2	14 C6
Connomara Mdw. TF4	17 E6
Conroy Dri. TF4	17 F4
Constable Dri. TF5	5 E4
Constitution Hill. TF1	11 H2
Cooke Dri. TF4	21 H2
Cooper Clo. TF2	15 E6
Copper Beech Rd. TF1	12 D3
Copperfield Dri. TF2	8 D4
Coppice Clo. TF7	26 B1
Coppice Dri. TF6	14 C2
Corbett Clo. TF4	21 F3
Cordingley Way. TF2	8 B6
Corfield Cres. TF2	13 H3
Cornbrook. TF3	22 C2
Coronation Cres. TF7	22 A5
Coronation Dri. TF2	8 D4
Cote Rd. TF5	5 E4
Cottage Clo. TF7	26 B1
Cottage Farm Clo. TF4	22 A6
Cound Clo. TF1	11 F1
Court Rd. TF7	22 A5
Court St. TF7	22 A5
Courtland Dri. TF2	8 A6
Cranage Cres. TF1	11 F3
Cranmere. TF3	22 D2
*Crawstone Clo, Fireclay Dri. TF2	14 C3
Crescent Rd, Hadley. TF1	12 C3
Crescent Rd, Wellington. TF1	11 G2
Crest Rd. TF2	15 E4
Cricketers La. TF2	14 D4
Croft Fold. TF2	17 F4
Crossbank. TF3	22 D1
Crosskeys La. TF1	12 D2
Crowdale Rd. TF5	5 E4
Crown St, Dawley. TF4	17 G6
Crown St, Wellington. TF1	11 G3
Cuckoo Oak Green.TF7	22 B5
Cuckoos Rest. TF4	21 H4
Culmington. TF3	22 C1
Cumberland Clo. TF12	24 D5
Cumberland Mews. TF1	12 C2
Curie Croft. TF3	6 B6
Curlew Dri. TF1	12 C1
Cygnet Dri. TF3	22 C3
Cyril Hayward Ct. TF1	13 E2
Daddlebrook. TF3	18 C4
Daisy Bank Dri. TF2	14 D3
Dalby Clo. TF1	12 B1
Dale Acre Way. TF3	3 C4
Dale End. TF8	24 C1
Dale Rd. TF8	24 C1
Dalelands. TF3	3 D4
Dalford Ct. TF3	3 C4
Dallamoor. TF3	18 C3
Damson Dri. TF3	13 G6
Danesford. TF3	3 D4
Darby Rd. TF8	20 B4
Dark La. TF3	25 E5
Dark Lane Dri. TF3	3 A6
Darliston. TF3	18 C4
Darwin Rd. TF1	11 G1
Dawley Bank. TF4	17 F4
Dawley Green Way. TF4	17 G3
Dawley Rd. TF1	12 B4
Dawley Way. TF4	17 G6
Daywell. TF3	18 C3
Dean Clo. TF2	14 D5
Dee Clo. TF1	5 G6
Deepdale. TF3	3 D5
Deepfield Rd. TF4	21 F2
Deer Park Rd. TF1	11 F1
Deercote. TF3	3 C4
Delamere Clo. TF3	17 E1
Delbury Ct. TF3	3 C4
Delphside. TF12	25 E5
Derwent Dri. TF3	14 D6
Deuxhill Clo. TF4	17 G4
Dickens Rd. TF2	8 B6
Dinchope Dri. TF3	3 D4
Dinthill. TF3	18 C4
Doddington. TF3	18 C4
Doddlecote Clo. TF3	22 B2
Dodmoor Grange. TF3	18 C5
Domas Way. TF4	17 F4
Donnerville Clo. TF1	11 E1
Donnerville Gdns. TF5	11 E1
Donnington Dri. TF2	8 B1
Donnington Way. TF2	8 C2
Donnington Wood Way. TF2	8 D4
Dorran Pl. TF2	14 C5
Doseley Rd. TF4	21 E1
*Dothill Ct, Breidden Pl. TF1	5 F6
Dove Ct. TF8	25 E2
Dovedale Fold. TF4	17 H5
Dovehouse Ct. TF12	25 E6
Downemead. TF3	3 D4
Downton Court. TF3	3 C5
Drapers Ct. TF1	11 G2
Draycott. TF3	3 D5
Drayton Way. TF4	17 F4
Drummery La. TF6	10 C2
Duckett Dri. TF4	21 F1
Dudmaston. TF3	18 D3
Duffryn. TF3	3 D4
Duke St, Broseley. TF12	24 D4
Duke St, St Georges. TF2	14 C4
Duke St, Wellington. TF1	11 G3
Dukes Hill. TF2	14 A5
Dukes Pl. TF2	14 C4
Dukes Way. TF2	14 C4
Dunlin Clo. TF1	12 C1
Dunmaster Way. TF3	22 A2
Dunsheath. TF3	3 C4
Dunstone. TF3	3 D4
Durrant Rd. TF2	14 C5
Duxmore Way. TF4	17 F4
Easthope Rd. TF12	24
Eaton Cres. TF2	14
Edinburgh Rd. TF12	24
Edward Parry Ct. TF4	17
Eglantine Clo. TF2	9
Eider Dri. TF1	6
Elderberry Clo. TF3	13
Elizabeth Cres. TF12	24
Elm Way. TF2	13
Elmpark Dri. TF1	11
Elmsdale Cres. TF5	4
Ely Clo. TF2	15
Emral Rise. TF1	5
Ennerdale Clo. TF2	12
Epsom Ct. TF1	12
Ercall Clo. TF2	13
Ercall Gdns. TF1	11
Ercall La. TF1	11
Ercall View. TF1	13
Essex Chase. TF2	15
Euston Way. TF3	3
Evelith La. TF11	23
Everglade Rd. TF2	14
Ewart Rd. TF2	8
Exeter Dri. TF1	12
Eyton Pl. TF4	17
Eyton Rd. TF4	17
Eyton View. TF1	5
Fairburn Rd. TF3	18
Fairfield Ct. TF1	11
Fairways Dri. TF7	25
Fallow Rd. TF5	
Far Vallens. TF1	13
Farm Clo. TF7	26
Farm La. TF4	16
Farm Lane Bungalows. TF2	8
Farm Lodge Gro. TF3	3
Farmstead Ct. TF1	1
Fellows Clo. TF4	21
Fence Rd. TF4	1
Fenns Cres. TF2	1
Ferndale Dri. TF2	18
Fernwood Clo. TF1	
Ferriday Clo. TF7	
Ferry Rd. TF8	26
Festival Gdns. TF1	1
Field Clo. TF4	
Field House Dri. TF2	
Field Rd. TF2	
Fieldfare Way. TF4	2
Fielding Clo. TF12	2
Fifth Av. TF2	
Finger Rd. TF4	2
Finsbury Dri. TF2	1
Fireclay Dri. TF1	1
Firecrest Dri. TF1	1
First Av. TF2	1
Flag Leasow. TF7	
Fleming Ct. TF1	
Floyer La. TF7	
Forest Clo. TF5	
Forester Gro. TF1	
Forester Rd. TF2	
Foresters Clo. TF4	
Forgegate. TF3	
Forsythia Clo. TF2	
Fosters Foel. TF4	
Foundry Ct. TF12	
Foundry La. TF12	
Fountain Dri. TF2	
Fourth Av. TF2	
Fowler Clo. TF1	
Fox Av. TF2	
Fox La. TF12	
Foxes Covert. TF5	
Foxglove Rise. TF3	
Frame La. TF3	21 H4
Freeston Av. TF2	25 G2
Frizes Leasowe. TF2	8 B5
Furnace La. TF2	14 A5

rnace Rd. TF2 14 B6
ingdales Dri. TF4 21 E1
field Rd. TF3 13 F6
insborough Way. TF5 5 E4
rbet Rd. TF4 21 G3
rden Clo. TF2 14 A2
tcombe Way. TF2 15 E5
te St. TF2 14 B4
tehouse Clo. TF1 5 H5
orge Chetwood Ct. TF4 17H5
orge Pl. TF1 11 F2
orge St, Dawley. TF4 17 F6
orge St,
  t Georges. TF2 14 C4
bons Clo. TF2 8 B6
bons Rd. TF2 8 B5
pin Rd. TF5 4 D6
well Gro. TF2 15 E5
tens Dri. TF4 21 G4
de Way. TF5 5 E4
dstone St. TF1 13 E2
be St. TF1 11 H3
belands. TF2 8 C5
n Cotts. TF2 13 F3
nbrook Rd. TF2 15 E5
ndale. TF4 16 D3
ndinning Way. TF7 25 G1
neagles Clo. TF7 26 B3
ucester Av. TF4 17 G5
ucester Ct. TF1 6 C5
vers Way. TF5 4 D4
oldney Ct,
  Great Western Dri. TF4 17 E6
f Links La. TF1 11 G5
och Clo. TF7 21 E6
odyear Way. TF2 8 D5
don Rd. TF2 8 A6
ugh Clo. TF2 15 E6
ilbourne Rd. TF2 14 C5
ver Clo. TF2 9 E3
ver St. TF2 14 C3
inger Dri. TF1 12 B1
mpian Clo. TF2 9 E3
nge Av. TF3 22 C1
nge Central. TF3 3 C4
nge La. TF2 15 F1
nge Rd. TF2 14 A6
nville Dri. TF2 9 E4
nville Rd. TF2 14 D1
nville St. TF2 14 C4
smere Clo. TF2 14 D6
vel Leasowes. TF4 21 F3
at Croft. TF3 17 F2
at Hay Dri. TF7 26 A3
at Western Dri. TF4 17 E6
ae Clo. TF3 22 C3
n Acres. TF2 13 G5
n Way. TF4 17 F4
naway Pl. TF2 8 B6
nfinch Clo. TF2 12 A1
ngage Way. TF2 8 D4
nlea Rd. TF2 14 A1
ley Clo. TF7 21 E6
hound Hill. TF2 14 A5
dle Rd. TF11 23 G6
shill Flats. TF1 5 F6
ourne Av. TF5 5 F4

on Pl. TF4 17 G4
ey Gdns. TF1 6 C5
ey Lodge Rd. TF1 13 F2
ey Park Rd. TF1 6 C5
ey Rd. TF2 13 F3

Hafren Rd. TF4 21 F3
Halcyon Ct. TF2 9 E4
Haldane. TF7 22 D2
Halifax Dri. TF1 6 C6
Hall Barn Clo. TF7 21 H6
Hall La. TF11 23 F6
Hall Park Way. TF3 3 A3
Halldene. TF1 12 C2
Hamilton Rd. TF4 21 G2
Hamlet Clo. TF2 13 H3
Hampton Hill. TF1 11 F5
Hancocks Dri. TF2 14 A5
Hanover Ct. TF7 22 A6
Harcourt. TF7 22 C6
Harding Clo. TF2 8 B5
Harebell Glade. TF3 18 D6
Harley Clo. TF1 5 F5
Harp La. TF4 21 G1
Harrington Heath. TF5 5 E4
Harris Grn. TF12 24 D5
Harris's La. TF8 25 E1
Harrison Clo. TF7 25 G1
Hartley Clo. TF3 13 F6
Hartsbridge Rd. TF2 13 G4
Harthill. TF2 13 G4
Hartshill Av. TF2 13 G4
*Hartshorn Ct,
  Meadow Rd. TF4 17 F5
Harvey Cres. TF1 12 C4
Harvington Clo. TF1 11 G1
Haughmond Ct. TF1 5 G6
Haughton Rd. TF11 19 G2
Hawksworth Rd. TF2 14 B6
Hawshaw Clo. TF3 18 B5
Hawthorn Pl. TF2 8 C4
Hawthorn Rd. TF2 8 C5
Haybridge Av. TF1 12 D2
Haybridge Hall Gdns. TF1 12 C2
Haybridge Rd. TF1 12 C3
Haybrook. TF7 23 E6
Haycocks Clo. TF1 5 F6
Hayes Rd. TF1 12 B5
Haygate Dri East. TF1 11 F4
Haygate Dri West. TF1 11 F4
Haygate Rd. TF1 11 E4
Hayward Av,
  Donnington. TF2 8 C5
Hayward Av,
  St Georges. TF2 14 C5
Hayward Par. TF2 13 H3
Hazel Way. TF2 14 B6
Hazelwood Dri. TF4 21 G3
Heath Hill. TF4 17 E4
Heath Rd. TF1 11 G1
Heather Dri. TF1 12 B3
Heatherdale. TF1 12 B1
Heathlands Clo. TF2 14 B4
Hem La. TF7 23 E3
Hendrie Clo. TF1 13 E4
Henley Dri. TF2 8 A6
Herbert Av. TF1 11 F4
Hereford Clo. TF2 15 F5
Hermitage Way. TF7 25 G1
Heron Clo. TF3 22 C4
Hertford Clo. TF1 12 A2
Hesba Clo. TF1 11 F3
Heslop. TF7 22 D3
Heywood
  Longsdale Ct. TF1 11 H3
Hiatt Av. TF1 11 H2
High Mount. TF2 8 C6
High St, Broseley. TF12 24 D5
High St, Dawley. TF4 17 F5
High St, Hadley. TF1 13 E2
High St, Ironbridge. TF8 24 D2
High St, Madeley. TF7 22 A6
High St, Wellington. TF1 11 H3
Highfields. TF4 16 D3
Highgrove Mdws. TF2 15 E5
Highland Lea. TF4 17 E6
Highway Way. TF1 12 C4

Hilda Hooke Clo. TF7 26 B1
Hill Crest Rd. TF2 14 C4
Hill Fold. TF4 17 F3
Hill Rd, Donnington. TF2 8 C1
Hill Rd, Overdale. TF2 13 F6
Hill St. TF2 14 C4
Hill Top Rd. TF2 13 G4
Hills Lane. TF7 22 B6
Hills Lane Dri. TF7 22 B6
Hillside. TF8 25 E2
Hillside Clo. TF1 12 B5
Hillside E. TF10 9 G1
Hillside Rd. TF2 14 A5
Hilton Clo. TF3 22 B2
Hilton Ter. TF2 14 B4
Hinkshay Rd. TF4 17 H6
Hockley Rd. TF12 24 D6
Hodge Bower. TF8 24 D1
Holland Dri. TF2 9 E4
Hollies Rd. TF1 11 F2
Hollinsgate. TF3 3 C3
Hollinswood Rd. TF2 3 C1
Holly Rd. TF4 21 F2
Hollybirch Gro.TF2 14 C5
Hollyhurst Rd. TF2 14 A2
Holme Clo. TF1 12 A1
Holmer Farm Rd. TF3 22 C2
Holmer La. TF3 22 C2
Holyhead Rd,
  Oakengates. TF2 3 D1
Holyhead Rd,
  Wellington. TF1 11 E4
Holywell La. TF4 21 E3
Hopeshay Clo. TF3 22 B2
Hopkins Heath. TF5 5 E4
Hordley Rd. TF1 11 F1
Hornbeam Clo. TF1 12 C4
Horne Rd. TF2 8 C1
Hornet Way. TF3 13 G6
Horse Chestnut Dri. TF5 5 F4
Horsehay Common. TF4 17 E5
Horton La, Horton. TF1 7 F2
Horton La, Trench. TF1 7 G6
Horton Rd. TF2 7 G6
Horton Wood. TF1 7 F5
Hoskins Clo. TF4 17 F5
Houseman Clo. TF3 21 H3
Houston Clo. TF1 14 C3
Howle Clo. TF3 22 B2
Hudson Clo. TF2 14 B2
Humber La. TF2 8 A1
Humber Way. TF2 8 A2
Huntsman Way. TF4 17 F4
Hurleybrook Way. TF1 12 C2
Hurst Clo. TF12 25 F6
Hutchinson Way. TF1 13 E4
Hyde Clo. TF2 9 E4

INDUSTRIAL ESTATES:
Castle Trading Est. TF2 3 C1
Central Park. TF2 14 B6
Heath Hill Ind Est. TF4 17 E5
Ketley Ind Est. TF1 13 E4
Priorslee Trading
  Est. TF2 3 C1
St Georges Rd Ind
  Est. TF2 14 C1
Telford Bri. Retail
  Park. TF3 3 A2
Telford Science &
  Technology Park. TF3 19 E5
Ice House Clo. TF1 5 H5
Innes Av. TF2 13 H4
Iris Cres. TF2 14 C2
Ironbridge By-Pass. TF4 20 C3
Ironbridge Rd,
  Broseley.TF12 25 E3
Ironbridge Rd,
  Madeley. TF7 21 F6
Ironmasters Way. TF3 3 B2
Ivatt Clo. TF4 21 H2

Ivor Thomas Rd. TF2 14 C5
Ivy Gro. TF1 11 F3
Ivy House Paddocks. TF1 13 E3
Jabe Davies Clo. TF2 14 C6
Jackson Av. TF12 24 D5
James Clay Ct. TF1 12 D3
James Clo. TF2 8 A6
James Nelson Cres. TF2 8 B5
James WayTF2 8 B5
Japonica Dri. TF1 6 C5
Jasmine Clo. TF3 13 F6
Jay Dri. TF1 12 A1
Jiggers Bank. TF8 20 C3
Jockey Bank. TF8 25 E2
John Broad Av. TF1 12 B4
Johnstone Clo. TF2 14 C2
Johnstone Rd. TF4 17 G5
Joseph Rich Av. TF7 21 H6
Jubilee Av. TF2 8 C4
Juniper Dri. TF2 13 H2
*Kearton Ter,
  Hadley Lodge Rd. TF1 13 F2
Keepers Cres. TF2 14 D3
Kemberton Dri. TF7 22 C6
Kemberton Rd. TF7 22 C5
Kemberton Way. TF7 22 C4
Kestrel Ct. TF1 12 B1
Kesworth Dri. TF2 15 E6
Ketley Town. TF1 13 E5
Ketley Vallens. TF1 13 E3
King St, Broseley. TF12 24 D4
King St, Dawley. TF4 17 G5
King St, Wellington. TF1 11 G2
Kings Haye Rd. TF1 11 G4
Kingsland. TF1 12 B4
Kingsley Dri. TF2 8 C3
Kingston Rd. TF2 14 A1
Kingsway Cres. TF1 12 B4
Knightsbridge Cres. TF3 22 A2
Knowle Wood View. TF3 18 C5
Laburnum Dri. TF7 26 A1
Laburnum Rd. TF2 14 A2
Ladbrook Dri. TF2 14 B5
Ladycroft. TF1 11 G2
Ladygrove. TF4 17 F4
Ladywood. TF8 24 D2
Lambeth Dri. TF3 22 A3
Lancaster Av. TF4 17 G5
Lancaster Pl. TF4 17 G5
Landy Clo. TF2 8 C2
Laneside. TF2 9 E3
Langer Ct. TF2 14 C4
Langholm Grn. TF7 25 G1
Langley Cres. TF4 17 G6
Langley Fold. TF4 17 G6
Lapwing Gate. TF2 14 D6
Larch Wood. TF3 18 C6
Lark Rise. TF2 14 C3
Larkspur Glade. TF3 18 C6
Laurel La. TF3 13 F6
Lawford Clo. TF4 21 G4
Lawley Central. TF3 3 B3
Lawndale. TF2 8 B5
Lawns Wood. TF3 3 A5
Lawrence Rd. TF1 11 F3
Lawton Farm Clo. TF1 6 C6
Lawton Farm Way. TF1 6 C6
Lea Ct. TF1 12 A1
Lea Dingle. TF1 25 G2
Leadon Clo. TF4 21 F3
Leaton Dri. TF1 11 F1
Leegate Av. TF1 6 C5
Leegomery Rd. TF1 11 G2
Lees Farm Dri. TF7 25 G1
Leeses Clo. TF5 5 E4
Legges Hill. TF12 24 D4
Legges Way. TF7 26 A2

Leicester Way. TF1 12 C1
Lennock Rd. TF2 8 B5
Leonard Clo. TF2 8 B5
Leonard St. TF2 14 A4
Leveson Clo. TF2 14 B3
Ley Brook. TF2 13 G4
Lhen Clo. TF2 9 E4
Lightmoor Rd. TF7 21 F4
Lilac Clo. TF3 13 G6
Lilyhurst Rd. TF10 9 F2
Lime Tree Way. TF1 12 A1
Limekiln Bank. TF2 14 D4
Limekiln La. TF1 12 A4
Lincoln Cres. TF2 14 A2
Lincoln Hill. TF8 24 C2
Lincoln Rd. TF2 14 A3
Linden Av. TF1 11 F3
Linden Gro. TF1 11 F3
Linden Ter. TF3 13 F6
Lindfield Dri. TF1 11 F2
Lineton Clo. TF2 8 A6
Linley Dri. TF3 22 B2
Lion St. TF2 14 A4
Lloyds Head. TF8 25 F3
Lodge La, Benthall. TF12 24 C5
Lodge La, Ironbridge. TF8 24 D1
Lodge Rd, Donnington. TF2 14 C1
Lodge Rd, St Georges. TF2 14 D4
Lodgewood La. TF2 15 E4
London Rd. TF2 14 C5
Long Lane Dri. TF7 21 E5
Long Meadow. TF3 18 C6
Longford Rise. TF1 12 A1
*Longmyrd Ct, Breidden Pl. TF1 5 F6
Longnor Rd. TF1 11 F1
Lord Murray Dri. TF7 21 G5
Lords Dri. TF2 14 D4
Low Valley Clo. TF1 13 E3
Lowe Ct. TF1 11 H3
Lower Brook. TF3 17 F2
Lower Dingle. TF7 25 G2
Lower Park Dri. TF1 5 F5
Lower Wood. TF3 17 F2
Loweswater Clo. TF2 14 D6
Lowry Clo. TF5 5 E4
Lucerne Clo. TF1 12 D2
Ludford Dri. TF3 22 B2
Ludlow Dri. TF3 22 B2
Lydbury Clo. TF3 22 C2
Lyndhurst Dri. TF2 8 A6

McCormick Dri. TF1 5 F5
McLean Dri. TF2 15 E5
Maddocks. TF7 22 A6
Maddocks Ct. TF1 11 H3
Madebrook Clo. TF7 26 C1
Madeley Rd. TF8 25 E2
Madeley Wood Vw. TF7 25 G2
Mafeking Dri. TF2 14 C2
Mafeking Rd. TF1 12 D2
Mafeking Ter. TF2 14 B2
Magna Clo. TF4 21 G2
Magnolia Dri. TF3 13 F6
Main Rd. TF2 13 G5
Majestic Way. TF4 21 G3
Malinsgate. TF3 3 A4
Mallory Dri. TF3 21 H3
Malvern Cres. TF4 21 F2
Manchester Dri. TF1 6 C5
Mannerley La. TF3 13 F6
Manor Dri. TF2 14 B5
Manor Gdns. TF4 21 G1
Manor Rise. TF1 12 C4
Manor Road, Arleston. TF1 12 C5
Manor Road, Hadley. TF1 12 D2
Manor Road, Little Dawley. TF4 21 F1

Manse Clo. TF1 12 D2
Manse Rd. TF1 12 D2
Mansell Rd. TF1 11 F3
Maple Clo. TF2 13 H2
Maple Wood. TF3 18 C6
Market Sq. TF1 11 G3
Market St, Oakengates. TF2 14 A4
Market St, Wellington, TF1 11 G3
Marlborough Way. TF3 17 E1
Marlow Dri. TF2 8 A6
Marquis Ter. TF2 14 A6
Marrions Hill. TF2 14 C4
Marsh Meadow Clo. TF1 5 F5
Marshbrook Way. TF2 9 E4
Mart Av. TF2 14 C5
Martin Rd. TF1 11 F3
Marton Dri. TF1 11 F1
Mason Dri. TF7 21 G6
Matlock Av. TF4 17 H5
Maurice Lee Av. TF1 13 H3
Mayfield. TF7 21 H6
Maypole Rd. TF12 24 D3
Mead Croft. TF2 21 H6
Meadow Clo, Madeley. TF7 26 B1
Meadow Clo, Trench. TF2 7 G6
Meadow Lea. TF7 22 A6
Meadow Rd, Dawley. TF4 17 F5
Meadow Rd, Muxton. TF2 8 D4
Meadow Rd, Wellington. TF1 11 E5
Meadowsweet Dri. TF2 15 E6
Medlar Clo. TF3 13 G6
Meese Clo. TF1 11 G1
Melbourne Clo. TF4 17 H5
Mellor Clo. TF7 25 G1
Melrose Gdns. TF1 11 F3
Mendip Clo. TF4 21 F2
Mercia Dri. TF1 12 B2
Mere Gro. TF5 5 F4
Merridale Cres. TF1 11 H2
Merrington Rd. TF2 9 E3
Meyrick Rd. TF1 11 G1
Middle Rd. TF2 14 A2
Mill Bank. TF1 12 A3
Mill Farm Dri. TF3 18 D5
Mill La, Broseley. TF12 24 D5
Mill La, Kemberton. TF11 23 G6
Mill La, Wellington. TF1 12 B3
Mill Way. TF2 7 H6
Millers Way. TF2 9 E4
Millfields Rd. TF1 12 B3
Millstream Way. TF1 6 D6
Milners Ct. TF1 17 F3
Milners La. TF4 17 F3
Milton Dri. TF7 21 G6
Milward Clo. TF2 8 B5
Mimosa Clo. TF7 26 A2
Miners Mdw. TF12 25 E6
Mitchel Way. TF7 21 G6
Mole Way. TF5 5 F5
Monet Clo. TF5 5 E5
Montgomery Mws. TF1 6 C5
Montgomery Rd. TF1 11 F3
Moor Rd. TF4 17 G5
Moorland Dri. TF2 15 E6
Morden Clo. TF2 14 B4
Morgan Way. TF1 13 E4
Morris Dri. TF2 8 C4
Morville Dri. TF1 5 F6
Mosclay Rd. TF2 14 C5
Moss Rd. TF2 14 C2
Mossey Green Way. TF1 13 G5
Mossey Grn. TF2 13 G5
Mound Way. TF7 21 G6
Mount Gilbert. TF1 12 B4
Mount Pleasant. TF2 14 A5
Mount Pleasant Dri. TF3 22 A4
Mount Pleasant Rd. TF7 26 B1

Mount Rd. TF4 17 G4
Mount Side. TF1 13 F5
Mount View Rd. TF2 14 A5
Mounts Clo. TF7 26 B1
Mulberry Ct. TF1 12 D2
Mullinder Dri. TF2 13 H6
Musk Rose Clo. TF2 8 D4
Muxton La. TF2 9 E3
Myford. TF4 20 D2
Nabb Clo. TF2 14 C4
Naird La. TF3 18 D6
Near Vallens. TF1 13 E2
Nelson Ct. TF1 11 H3
Nelson Way. TF2 9 E3
Nevil Rd. TF1 11 F2
New Bridge. TF8 25 F2
New Bridge Rd. TF8 25 E2
New Church Rd. TF1 11 H4
New Hall Rd. TF1 11 H3
New Rd, Donnington. TF2 8 C5
New Rd, Ironbridge. TF8 24 D2
New Rd, Little Dawley. TF4 21 G1
New Rd, Madeley. TF7 26 B1
New Rd, Wrockwardine Wood. TF2 14 A2
New St, Dawley. TF4 17 G6
New St, Oakengates. TF2 14 A4
New St, St Georges. TF2 14 B4
New St, Wellington. TF1 11 G3
New Town. TF4 17 G5
New Trench Rd. TF2 7 G6
Newbrookdale. TF1 12 D2
Newcomen Way. TF7 21 E6
Newfield Dri. TF2 14 A1
Newtonmere Dri. TF1 11 F2
Nickless Way. TF4 17 F4
Nightingale Way. TF1 6 B6
Norfield Dri. TF3 18 D5
North Rd. TF1 11 F2
North St. TF2 14 B4
Northwood Ter. TF3 22 B1
Norton Dri. TF3 22 A2

Paddock Ct. TF4 17
Paddock La. TF11 23
Padmans Alley. TF12 24
Pageant Dri. TF4 21
Panorama. TF2 14
Paradise. TF8 24
Parish Clo. TF4 21
Park Av. TF7 22
Park Clo. TF2 14
Park Ct. TF7 21
Park La. TF3 17
Park Lane Av. TF7 21
Park Rd, Donnington. TF2 8
Park Rd, Malinslee. TF4 17
Park St, Madeley. TF7 21
Park St, Wellington. TF1 11
Park View. TF8 25
Parkdale. TF1 12
Parklands. TF1 12
Parkway. TF7 21
Partridge Clo. TF1 12
Pasmore Clo. TF3 21
Pasteur Dri. TF1 6
Pavilion Clo. TF 14
Pearson Rd. TF2 14
Pemberton Rd. TF5 4
Pembridge Clo. TF2 8
Pembridge Dri. TF1
Pendil Clo. TF1 11
Penistone Clo. TF2 8
Peregrine Way. TF1 6
Perivale Gdns. TF2 9
Perry Ct. TF1 11
Peters Clo. TF4 21
Peveril Bank. TF4 17
Picasso Clo. TF5 9
Pickering Rd. TF2 8
Pickstock Clo. TF3 22
Picton Clo. TF2 14
Pine View. TF2 8
Pinewood Av. TF2 8
Pintail Dri. TF1
Pitchford Dri. TF2 11
Plough Rd, Wrockwardine Wood. TF2 14
Plough Rd, Wellington. TF1 11
Plover Gate. TF1
Pool Clo. TF2
Pool Farm La. TF1
Pool Hill. TF4 2
Pool Hill Rd. TF4 1
Pool Meadow. TF1 1
Pool Rd. TF2 1
Pool Side. TF2 1
Pool View. TF4 1
Poplar Clo. TF7 1
Poplar Dri. TF1 1
Poppy Dri. TF2
Portley Rd. TF4 1
Portobello Clo. TF3 1
Pound La. TF12 2
Powder La. TF2
Powell Rd. TF2 1
Powis Dri. TF1 1
Powis Pl. TF4 1
Prestage Clo. TF12 1
Preston Gro. TF2 1
*Priestland Ter, Furnace La. TF2
Primmer Rd. TF2
Primrose Gro. TF1
Prince Andrew Dri. TF3
Prince Charles Cres. TF3
Prince Edward Cres. TF3
Prince St. TF7
Princes End. TF2
Princes St. TF1 14 A4
Princess Anne Gdns. TF4 9 E5
Princess Av. TF1
Priors Lee Rd. TF11 11 F2

Tadorna Dri. TF3 — 22 C2
Talbot Clo. TF2 — 14 B1
Talbot Rd. TF2 — 14 B1
Tamarisk Clo. TF3 — 13 G6
Tan Bank. TF1 — 11 G3
Tarbach Clo. TF12 — 25 F6
Teagues Cres. TF2 — 13 G1
Tee Lake Boulevard. TF1 — 5 E5
Teece Dri. TF2 — 15 E6
Telford Rd,
  Dawley Bank. TF4 — 17 H4
Telford Rd,
  Wellington. TF1 — 11 F5
Telford Rd. TF3 — 3 D3
Teme Av. TF1 — 5 F6
Tenbury Dri. TF2 — 8 A6
Teresa Way. TF1 — 6 B6
Tern Clo. TF4 — 21 F3
Tern Way. TF1 — 11 G1
The Avenue,
  Benthall. TF12 — 24 B5
The Avenue,
  Wrockwardine. TF6 — 10 B2
The Beaches. TF5 — 4 D6
The Bentlands. TF1 — 24 C4
The Brambles. TF3 — 17 G2
The Bungalows. TF2 — 8 D4
The Cloisters. TF2 — 13 H3
The Close. TF8 — 20 C4
The Common. TF2 — 8 C5
The Court. TF7 — 26 A3
The Crescent. TF2 — 8 C4
The Crofts. TF7 — 21 E5
The Delph. TF3 — 18 B6
The Fields. TF2 — 8 D5
The Foxes. TF7 — 26 A2
The Grove Est. TF2 — 14 C5
The Hay. TF3 — 17 F2
The Incline. TF1 — 13 F5
The Knowle. TF8 — 25 F3
The Lawns. TF1 — 11 G2
The Ley. TF4 — 21 G1
The Lloyds. TF8 — 25 F2
The Meadows,
  Ketley Bank. TF2 — 13 H5
The Meadows,
  Lawley. TF4 — 16 D3
The Mines. TF12 — 24 D3
The Nabb. TF2 — 14 B3
The Paddock. TF2 — 9 E4
The Parade,
  Donnington. TF2 — 8 C5
The Parade,
  Wellington. TF1 — 11 G3
The Pippins. TF3 — 18 C6
The Rock. TF3 — 17 F1
The Rookery. TF7 — 22 A6
The Savannahs. TF1 — 5 G5
The Square. TF8 — 24 D2
The Stables. TF2 — 9 E4
The Stockings. TF4 — 21 E3
The Timbers. TF2 — 14 C3
The Wharfage. TF8 — 24 C1
The Woodlands. TF2 — 14 B2
Third Av. TF2 — 3 B1
Thirlmere Gro. TF2 — 14 D6
Thistle Clo. TF3 — 18 C5
Thornton Park Av. TF4 — 9 E4
Toll Rd. TF1 — 12 B5
Tontine Hill. TF8 — 24 D2
Trafalgar Clo. TF1 — 8 D3
Trench Clo. TF2 — 7 G6
Trench Lock. TF1 — 13 F1

Trench Lock 1. TF1 — 13 F1
Trench Lock 2. TF1 — 13 F1
Trench Lock 3. TF1 — 13 G1
Trench Lock 5. TF1 — 13 G2
Trench Rd. TF2 — 7 G6
Trenleigh Gdns. TF2 — 13 H1
Trinity Rd. TF4 — 21 F2
Trinity View. TF1 — 13 H5
Troon Way. TF7 — 26 B3
Tudor Meadow. TF2 — 7 G6
Turbervill Clo. TF2 — 14 D3
Turnpike Ct. TF2 — 14 C4
Turnstone Dri. TF1 — 12 C2
Turreff Av. TF2 — 8 C4
Tweedale Court. TF7 — 22 B5
Tweedale Cres. TF7 — 22 B5
Tweedale North. TF7 — 22 B5
Tweedale South. TF7 — 22 B5
Tynsley Ct. TF7 — 22 A6
Tynsley Ter. TF7 — 22 A6

Ullswater Clo. TF2 — 14 C6
Undertrees Clo. TF1 — 5 G5
Underwood. TF12 — 25 E4
Union Ct. TF1 — 13 E2
Union Rd,
  Wellington. TF1 — 11 G4
Union Rd, Wrockwardine
  Wood. TF2 — 14 A2
Union St. TF1 — 13 E2
Uplands Av. TF2 — 13 H3
Upper Dingle. TF7 — 25 F2
Upper Rd. TF7 — 22 A6
Upper Wood. TF3 — 17 F2
Urban Gdns. TF1 — 12 B3
Urban Rd. TF2 — 14 A2
Urban Villas. TF2 — 14 C4
Urban Way. TF1 — 12 B3

Valley Rd, Arleston. TF1 — 12 B5
Valley Rd, Overdale. TF3 — 17 F1
Verbena Way. TF7 — 26 A2
Vicar St. TF2 — 13 H4
Victoria Av, Ketley. TF1 — 12 D3
Victoria Av,
  Wellington. TF1 — 11 H3
Victoria Ct. TF1 — 13 E2
Victoria Rd, Madeley. TF7 — 21 H6
Victoria Rd,
  Wellington. TF1 — 11 G3
Victoria St. TF1 — 11 H3
Viewlands Dri. TF2 — 8 A5
Villa Ct. TF7 — 22 A6
Village Ct. TF2 — 18 D1
Vineyard Dri. TF1 — 11 G2
Vineyard Rd. TF1 — 11 G2
Violet Clo. TF2 — 9 E4
Viscount Av. TF4 — 21 H3

Wade Rd. TF2 — 14 B1
Wadham Clo. TF1 — 12 A1
Waggoners Fold. TF3 — 17 H4
Wagtail Dri. TF4 — 21 H3
Walder Clo. TF4 — 17 F5
Walker Cres. TF2 — 14 B3
Walker St. TF1 — 11 G3
Walney Ct. TF7 — 21 F6
Walsh Clo. TF2 — 15 E5
Walton Av. TF6 — 13 H3
Waltondale. TF7 — 21 G6
Wantage. TF7 — 21 G5
Warrensway. TF7 — 21 E6
Waterloo Clo. TF1 — 13 E3

Waterloo Rd, Ketley. TF1 — 13 E2
Waterloo Rd,
  Wellington. TF1 — 11 H3
Waterloo St. TF8 — 25 E2
Watling St. TF1 — 12 B4
Waverley. TF7 — 21 G5
Wavertree Clo. TF2 — 14 B4
Waxhill Clo. TF2 — 8 D6
Wayside. TF7 — 21 G6
Wealdstone. TF7 — 21 F5
Weavers Rise. TF2 — 13 H5
Webb Cres. TF4 — 21 F1
Wedgewood Cres. TF1 — 12 D3
Weir Gdns. TF1 — 13 E1
Wellington Rd,
  Admaston. TF5 — 4 D6
Wellington Rd,
  Coalbrookdale. TF8 — 20 C5
Wellington Rd,
  Donnington. TF2 — 8 B4
Wellington Rd,
  Lawley. TF4 — 16 D3
Wellsfield. TF7 — 21 G5
Wellswood Av. TF2 — 3 B1
Wenlock Ct. TF7 — 21 F6
Wesley Dri. TF2 — 13 H5
Wesley Rd. TF8 — 25 E2
West Av. TF2 — 8 B5
West Centre Way. TF4 — 17 G2
West Rd,
  Ketley Bank. TF2 — 13 G5
West Rd, Wellington. TF1 — 11 F3
West St. TF2 — 14 C4
West View Ter. TF7 — 21 G6
Westbourne. TF7 — 21 F6
Westerdale Clo. TF4 — 21 F1
Westerkirk Dri. TF7 — 25 G1
Western Rise. TF1 — 12 D3
Westmorland Mews. TF1 — 12 C2
Weston Dri. TF1 — 11 F2
Weybridge. TF7 — 21 E6
Weyman Rd. TF1 — 11 F1
Wharf Clo. TF2 — 14 B4
Wheatley Cres. TF1 — 6 D6
Wheeldale Clo. TF4 — 21 E1
Whimbrel Clo. TF1 — 12 C1
Whinchat Clo. TF1 — 12 B1
Whitchurch Dri,
  Shawbirch. TF1 — 5 G5
Whitchurch Dri,
  Wellington. TF1 — 12 A1
Whitchurch Rd. TF1 — 11 G1
White Horse Clo. TF8 — 17 F4
Whitebeam Clo. TF3 — 17 G1
Whitehall Gdns. TF12 — 25 E6
Whitemere Rd. TF1 — 11 F2
Whitington Clo. TF2 — 14 A3
Whitmore Clo. TF12 — 25 F6
Whitworth Dri. TF3 — 18 B6
Wicket Clo. TF2 — 14 D4
Widewaters Clo. TF4 — 21 G3
Wigmores. TF7 — 21 G5
Wild Thyme Dri. TF2 — 8 D4
Wildwood. TF7 — 21 F5
Wilkinson Av. TF12 — 25 E6
Willetts Way. TF4 — 17 F4
Williams Rd. TF2 — 8 C2
Willow Bank. TF4 — 21 H3
Willow Rd. TF2 — 14 B4
Willowfield. TF7 — 21 G5
Wilmere Ct. TF7 — 21 F6
Winchester Dri. TF2 — 9 F4
Windermere Dri. TF2 — 14 C6

Windsor Cres. TF12
Windsor Pl. TF4
Windsor Rd, Arleston. TF1
Windsor Rd, Dawley. TF4
Winifreds Dri. TF2
Winston Dri. TF2
Withybrook. TF7
Withywood Dri. TF3
Wolverley Ct. TF7
Wombridge Rd,
  Trench. TF2
Wombridge Rd,
  Wombridge. TF2
Wombridge Way. TF2
Wood Clo. TF2
Woodbine Clo. TF2
Woodcroft. TF7
Woodford Grn. TF5
Woodhall Clo. TF5
Woodhouse. TF2
Woodhouse Central. TF3
Woodhouse Clo. TF2
Woodhouse Cres. TF2
Woodhouse La,
  Horsehay. TF4
Woodhouse La,
  Priorslee. TF2
Woodhouse La,
  Redhill. TF2
Woodhouse Rd. TF12
Woodland Villas. TF2
Woodlands Av. TF1
Woodlands Clo. TF12
Woodlands Grn. TF12
Woodlands La. TF4
Woodlands Rd. TF8
Woodpecker Clo. TF1
Woodrows. TF7
Woodrush Heath. TF3
Woodside. TF8
Woodside Av. TF7
Woodside Clo. TF1
Woodside Rd. TF1
Woodwell. TF1
Woollam Rd. TF1
Worcester Rd. TF4
Wordsworth Way. TF2
Worfe Clo. TF3
Wrekin Clo. TF2
Wrekin Dri. TF2
Wrekin Rd. TF1
Wrekin View,
  Madeley. TF7
Wrekin View,
  Wrockwardine. TF6
Wrens Nest La. TF1
Wrockwardine Rd. TF1
Wrockwardine Wood
  Way. TF2
Wroxeter Way. TF3
Wych Elm Dri. TF5
Wyke La. TF12
Wyke Rise. TF1
Wyvern. TF7
Yates Way. TF2
Yellowstone Clo. TF2
Yew Tree Dri. TF10
Yew Tree Rd. TF7
York Rd. TF2

PLEASE NOTE: All maps, plans and indexes contained in this publication are strictly copyright. They may not be copied or reproduced in any way with prior permission of both Estate Publications and the Ordnance Survey.

Postcodes have been reproduced with permission of the Post Office. Every care has been taken by Estate Publications but the Post Office cannot be responsible for any errors or omissions. The outward part of the Postcode which is reproduced in this index will not suffice in identifying a particular addr The list of Postcodes is a copyright work of the Post Office.

Edition 319 F 1C